FOOTPRINTS

FOOTPRINTS

A COLLECTION OF POEMS AND PROSE

FAMO MUSA

Review Journal Publications

Home but Temporary as a "Waiting Room" published in The People Have Spoken Zine. City College. Class Volume 1. 2018

What Makes a Home published by City Works Literary Journal, Vol. 26. 2019.

Own it! Published by City Works Literary Journal, Vol. 26. 2019. And Acorn Review Literary Magazine 2019.

Mars Here We Come published by City Works Literary Journal, Vol. 27. 2020.

ISBN - 979-8-218-37626-0

Library of Congress Control Number: 2024904834

Illustrations by Halima_Illustrations

Cover Designer by Jmar Creative Studio

Edited by Bramble & Crow Books

For more information:

Instagram: https://www.instagram.com/famoswriting/

For my parents
For my children
For my community
For my 12-year-old self

CONTENTS

"If you don't see the book you want on the shelf,
write it."

-Beverly Cleary

Introduction

-The reasons I write

I never felt more powerless and unheard than when I couldn't write or read in English. I felt mute and invisible as if no one could see me since I had no means of sharing myself. I was just existing. Floating with a dark cloud of creativity behind me, waiting for the sun to shine through it, without an inspiration to feed my soul. I learned how to read in high school; it felt like I was seeing the world for the first time. I now had the power to transport myself into different stories and dimensions. I could pause time and get into the characters' heads and walk through their stories. It took my family a while before they could understand why my ears didn't work when my face was buried in a book, for them to understand I wasn't there anymore. On top of that, after a while, I decided I wanted to do the same thing my favorite authors did, I wanted to live in pages, give someone the power to walk inside my head, and live in my imagination for a change. I longed to have my favorite authors' imagination and create worlds out of thin air.

I read everything that captures my attention, and I tend to lean towards science fiction fantasy, and romance, stories that would make me forget about my problems for a while. I write to escape reality and to unwind. My writing is therapeutic, a form of letting go and letting things out. I write to declutter my mind. After I write a piece, I'm light, I feel like I've shed a piece of me. I write everything: past stories, experiences, successes, and failures, passing thoughts, and things I go through. This collection is my life. You are holding my baby that I created from scratch– handle it with care. I want my readers to understand where I am coming from and what I'm trying to say, so my poetry and prose are not a mystery; I tell it the way it is, so there won't be any misunderstandings. I hope you get inspired and share a piece of yourself, if not publicly, at least with yourself.

1

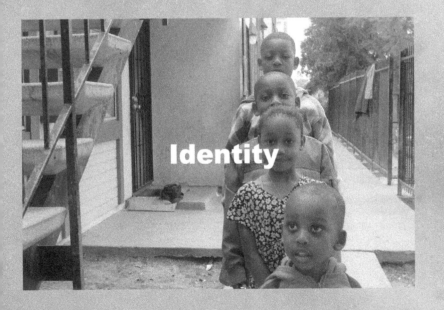

Identity

-My Birth

Some stories are like bullets to the essence

cutting to the core

my mother's tale of my birth was such a tale for me.

The tale of how I burst out of her sheltered womb

her pain-filled wounded screams echoing upon my arrival

surrounded by raisin bushes.

Death and destruction

with the wailing sounds of my cry

her salvation

hands cover both of our mouths to smother our screams

to keep the rebels lurking from hearing the echoes of new beginnings

I went months with no identity

like an insignificant caged bird

until the demise of my dear father

music of sorrow taking over

polluting the air

after days of mourning, finally,

his mother's name took his place.

I'm named, I have an identity, even if it took the death of someone beloved, I'm somebody, free to grow

my own wings.

-Own it!

It was like the Earth held its breath when I was finally named,

they called me, "God exists" while they decided what to name me,

when it came, its purpose blessed, it felt as if cursed,

as if, it flowed out from my grandma's lifeless body

and joined my soul, now it was my turn to take on the burden

to be a fiery woman.

I grew up in the desert forest of Kenya

running wild and lost like a transparent soul

with ripped clothes, tasked with chores thrice the weight

of an elephant resembling my wailing name

I live restless, and fearful dreams about life outside of myself

in my mind's eye, I see the life of a boy I so envy

so swift, so easy, impossible to catch.

I craved to return the life of a girl I was given

to hand back the blessing, the name I borrowed

to escape the lessons of what it took to become a woman

my strength entwined with weakness.

The weight of what makes a woman, supposedly

they spill shit out of their mouths, vomiting insults and imperfections.

To be timid but experienced, have craves but shed other body fat,

stay home, breed, and become a pleasure machine,

be candid and quiet, beautiful but humble

each demand with a burning sensation that fills the gut

but in my being,

I knew.

I am to be nurtured

as easily as I fell

I rise with both wings high

I am a warrior, my womb is home to the celestial

I am a goodness with immense mental power

blessed by Mother Nature.

Let my fire burn at your feet, for it has the power to bring life

my femininity contributes to humanity, it comes with a greater purpose

as effortless as the air that passes through the lungs.

I am black excellence, and my womanhood is not to be feared

it is an unexplored pyramid, elevated from three different countries

my beauty surface brilliance

my melanin untouchable.

As if you can live by anyone's beauty standards

as if your role was written in stone

to think any opinion could possibly matter.

I mean...I am a woman after all...I will always

rise like the ocean in a high tide.

-Unsaid

Silence speaks a thousand words, silent wrath, choking on words unsaid so many unspoken, sitting on my chest, words like

"I'm fading away"

the old me dying slowly, replaced by complacent, replaced with your version of me

"where am I?"

I loved me and I'm letting you chip me away, without a word

-Superstitions

Growing up, my mother would always tell us stories about back home,

some of the stories left us in cold sweat,

she used them to discipline us,

her favorites were about the people who ignore superstitions.

I was taught to be aware of black cats

they shed smoke of bad luck in their wake.

If I find a dead bird in front of my door, it is bad luck,

sent by somebody wishing me ill

this knowledge gave birth to ailurophobia and ornithophobia.

My mother also told me to never sit with my legs spread out,

if someone were to cross them,

they will transform their laziness on to me

I think she was training me to be a lady.

I can't sit between the door,

I might block angels from entering the house to bless me.

Sleep paralysis is the devil sitting on my chest and I extended the invitation,

the memory of such an invitation eludes me.

If I laugh at my uncle, I will get those small eye bumps as a punishment
my eye was pregnant with a stye all my life.

As a mother, I can't give my last or middle name to my children, that honor is left for the hereafter,

apparently, in life, it is the father's turn

they can only own my name in death.

I am not allowed to whistle at night,

the devil is a Mockingjay.

If a baby looks into a mirror, they will feast on their feces,

there is a festival of feces somewhere out there.

If a small tornado is heading my way,

all I need to do is point at it with my pinky,

and it will change direction or decimate.

The tornados in Texas will not halt at my pinky

another option is to recite a passage from the Quran,

or the devil in the tornado will sweep me off my feet

some days I want to be swept off my feet.

-Chasing Words

Not being able to speak English

was like being paralyzed

I could feel words trying to crawl out of my throat

but a steel wall blocked its path.

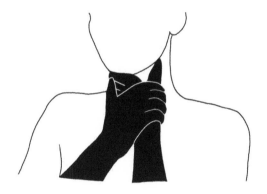

-Being Pulled in Two Directions

Being a teenager in America as a foreigner

was like being split in half,

two cultures entwined

I was expected to be a certain way,

like duality's sway

as if living a double life,

a complex ballet.

In one world, traditions deeply ingrained

in another, a lifestyle,

society unchained.

At home, ancestral customs, old tales, and cuisine

hold me tight

but at school just an American teenager

hiding my skirt and scarf in my backpack

carefree, striping rules, and friending boys.

My roots in constant conflict

like the moon during an eclipse

it can't decide if it's day or night

at times, I was proud of my heritage's grace

but often felt lost in a cultural maze

ensnared.

Footprints

My clothes made me unique and a target for bullies,

a fusion of cultures, like being in a trial to fit in

I was the bridge between worlds, in a cultural divide

like a straitjacket too tight

but I still had both worlds to guide me.

I yearned for acceptance,

to truly be accepted even if it was just in one world,

in a place where I felt wanted,

yet, in time, I discovered my strength lies within

as I learned to embrace the two worlds I was part of.

-Growing Up with Sisters

I ache for the chaos of nonsense screaming, the constant accusations of who stole who's baati[1]

the distancing of our parents when we felt wronged

"Your" father is acting up

"Your" mother is doing too much

the tag of war with the phone chargers and the world's most annoying question, "How much percent is your phone"?

"none of your beeswax, give me back my charger!"I miss the weekly random dancing, using YouTube videos to record ourselves, and saving them until the next year when we would finally post them as highlights as if that would take away the embarrassment.

I miss our arguments about whose turn it was to wash dishes, sweep the floor, or wash the bathroom, I think our mother grew gray hair with each argument. I miss you guys walking into my room like it was yours, and just dropping onto my bed, using my phone to record yourselves on my Snapchat.

I miss gathering in Mom's room for family meetings, crowding her bed, and I miss game nights, the Jenga with Dad, where the loser drinks raw eggs which was usually him.

I miss when the family would have their daily dose of comparing us to other kids who were "perfect" compared to our lazy selves and we would have our secret nonverbal conversations with eye rolls. How we couldn't wait to be adults and not have to worry about being told what to do and freedom! How stupid was that?

Now I wish I appreciated those moments. I feel the ache of our empty house miles away. I miss being surrounded by your echoes.

-My Self-diagnosed ADHD

I'm in the kitchen thawing meat for dinner

I find myself yearning to use the bathroom

on my way to the bathroom

I see a stain on the coffee table, I must clean it

with the Clorox wipes under the bathroom sink

good thing I'm heading that way.

In the bathroom, I find the wipes

next to a dirty hand towel that I must wash,

while washing the hand towel

I see white dots kissing the mirror

I use the Windex and the towel to clean the mirror,

behind the toilet and the tub.

After I'm done, I head to the kitchen to resume my cooking

in the process of washing the serving spoon I used,

I realize I still have to pee after hearing the sound of trickling water

now I must do the whole process again.

That's how my day goes every day.

So tell me, do I have ADHD like Google tells me

or is everyone doing the same thing?

-See Yourself

I don't see many words written by someone like me

I want to see myself on pages

since no one is doing it

I'm going to be the first

I hope you see yourself in my words.

-The Shape of Me

I grew up in City Heights, a loud and lively community in the heart of San Diego– but even with all its colors, food, and music, whenever I tell someone where I'm from, they'll usually ask, "What country is that?" Pick someone in La Jolla, and they'll have no idea what I'm talking about. That's how unknown the neighborhood was. Only folks from similar communities like Logan and Southeast would know of City Heights because of its ethnic diversity, or as others used to call it, the "ghetto," where low-income families, refugees, and immigrants "are dumped." For a time, City Heights was even considered to be violent and "for the poor," where police followed groups of young boys and girls just because they were huddled together. But it's not unsafe–and I knew that even as a little girl.

For me, City Heights is home, it's where my family and I settled when we first came to America in 2004. It is vibrant, like the beach at the peak of the day, and vivid, like the tower that represents the city. The rows of identical apartments surround mint-green trees that turn apricot copper during the fall. Sometimes we would use the trees to hang clothes we repurpose for cleaning rugs. It is where I used to climb the monkey bars using our next-door neighbor's stairs, who would then tell my mom every time I fell off. While dangling, I felt the roughness of the abrasive rock of the stairs against my palms, as if it were layered with scrapes under my sweaty palms.

It is where our house faces the elegant auburn ginger-colored mosque that looks like a low castle. Where the beautiful echo of the call of prayer *Adhan*, is peaceful to my ears, reminding my fellow Muslims that it is time to pray. The irresistible melodious voice fills the community every day, five times a day. Neighboring the mosque is a titian color Chinese temple with a hint of pearl tan that gives off the scent of incense every New Year. The fragrance of jasmine and rose populate the community, where it gets into people's houses through windows or under the door.

Every morning, I wake to the whiff of the aromatic incense by the taste of the floral and fruity tang in my throat. That is how close everyone is.

It is where we mix and mingle religions and traditions when it is time to celebrate. It is where colorful murals on buildings are labeled as graffiti by outsiders, to us it's art. You can walk a couple of blocks to eat Ethiopian, Chinese, Vietnamese, Japanese, Somali, or Mexican foods, and sometimes taco trucks play melodies down the street every five minutes switching from an ice cream truck to a food truck. Where a vendor that sells pillows yells in Spanish every Saturday and Sunday down the street. The aroma of the different foods coming from each apartment alone seems like it can feed many. I remember my taste buds celebrating after eating Carne Asanda fries from Taco Fiesta. You can hear the energy of the people living there vibrating in the air. This is the city I grew up in.

-Life as a Candle

I'm the flame who burns within, a warm wave.

As if the world is melting around me.

I rather be outside exploring the world,

I don't have anyone except for that match that ignites me.

I dream of lasting forever but it's wishful thinking.

As I wink out of existence, I worry I can never belong to just one special person.

I want others to think I matter, be a celestial wick.

The thought that I can never be reborn keeps me awake at night.

I make people feel calm and awaken their creativity.

I was once blown out while in use, a fading fire.

The fact that I ran out makes me feel vanquished.

My favorite time is nighttime as dusk awakens.

I like to bring people joy as an eternal flame,

and be the candle who burns out doubts.

-34 in Counting

34 years on this earth

what did I do for those 34 years?

I have loved

I have lost

I have loved again.

I dreamed, inspired, and led.

I breathed life into three angels who heard my cries.

I have thrived and failed.

34 years seems like a long time and yet no time at all

when cut short.

I wonder what is in store for me

for the next 34 years,

only time will tell.

-Running from Myself

Floating in the air

trying to escape the snake on the ground

as it stays on my trail

eating everything in its wake

I come back down in exhaustion

and it catches up to me

only to see the shadow of self-doubt.

2

Home

-My Kenya

My first love,

you've been in my mind lately.

My home away from home,

so far away

yet near at heart.

The vibrant and joyful people I left behind,

I remember cooking ugali and beans

in small cans,

which we reused as we played house.

Running around,

trying to find places to hide

as we seek with sweat running down our backs

a barefoot tomboy with ripped pants

running around the boiling ground.

The sounds of hyenas' laughter in the night.

The land of burning sands on cracked gravel

hot and baking

yet simple with life.

Rocky and spiky with thorny bushes

that produces lush plants

when it rains, once or twice a year.

I see you through the diamond stars of a clear sky

I can't wait for the day we meet in person

and walk through the memories we once made.

-My Ancestors

The beginning hardship

1830

years of movement

starvation, and drought

enticed by the promises

of jobs

of paradise

of distant lands

away from home

when the ruse failed

turned captive

farmers to laborers

assimilated

until 1960

freedom at last.

- Home but Temporary as a "Waiting Room"

Home.

Kakuma Refugee Camp. Kenya.

Neighborhoods, divided as blocks,

ours was block DB.

Mud brick houses,

wood, and cement blocks with tiny holes as windows and a side door,

roof of sheet metal, corrugated iron sheet

rows of houses surrounded by fencing made of thorns,

barb wires and trees.

Overcrowded, scorching, harsh, and dry.

Sandstorms, drought, and thorn bushes throughout,

exposed to the elements, cluttered, gritty earth with dirt tarps.

Humid but dry, so dry the ground is cracked,

footprints

sand and surplus weeds everywhere,

dusty unpaved roads.

Some people call it the "waiting room" purgatory,

temporary survival.

Footprints of generations abandoned.

But for my eleven-year-old-self,

it was home.

Brick mud bed, with mosquito nets,

only adults could use it.

Family of eight in one room,

kids slept on the floor with blankets.

Kakuma, harsh landscape.

desert for days.

no electricity, no ventilation,

no plumbing, no sewage.

kids "go" outside, and adults build homemade toilets.

not enough showers.

walking miles for water.

Sunny,

kids never boxed up inside.

unending games,

coming up with new games.

unconvincing

but still healthy African children.

Kids who are always together,

no one left behind

racing through the forest to collect firewood,

sprinting back home.

Sighting wild animals

we were invisible to the native half-dressed Turkana people.

Sunbathing

gazing at the arrangements of the ivory clouds,

looking for shapes in the sky

at night, looking for sparkling stars.

watching the pink-orange illumination of twilight.

Waking up to the chickens as an alarm clock,

to catch the yellow-orange milky luminosity of dawn.

After a downpour, which only happens once in a blue moon,

we'd play hide and seek in the tall mushy fertilized grass.

Running in the rain with laughter since the sun still burns,

yet it rains.

Going back to home after ages,

body heavy with fatigue,

it's dinner time,

time to catch a spot on the floor,

to sleep as if in a coma,

next to my five other siblings

and not feel a thing because

my tiny body passed out but still blissful,

I am home for the moment.

-My Room

Space

wide open space

small space

my space

lack of space

in a house full of people

hiding from socializing

while creating magic

lost in space in my mind

staring into space

enclosed space, but still sheltered

in my safe haven.

-Floating English

My words are from three different countries,

worlds intertwined,

with a melody of sounds I cannot grasp,

leaving me feeling lost in its vastness

chirping in my ears,

like a symphony.

English dances around,

yet the notes elude me,

keeping me bound, the words, linger,

stuck on my tongue, silent frustrations,

fighting to come out.

The languages are not merely letters and sounds,

they're bridges to connections that know no bounds

and yet my story unfurls, wanting to climb out

my thoughts, a surely swirl,

It took me four years of high school,

but the words broke free from their chains

releasing the beauty within, I see the barriers start to flow.

Finally, the voice in my new country finds me,

I am formed of words from three different countries

sewing me together, making me whole.

-What Makes a Home?

I was born in Somalia in 1990, where my ancestors were forced to be during the Arab Slave trade. My family fled Somalia in 1996 to Kenya, where they were in a refugee camp until 2004. By then, Kenya was facing starvation and famine, so the United Nations and the International Organization of Migration, the IOM, stepped in to help. The solution was to bring some of the refugees to the United States for a better life. I was 12 years old when my family resettled in the U.S.

Kakuma Refugee Camp is in Kenya. The neighborhoods were categorized into blocks. There were hundreds of them, which was the only way to tell them apart because they ran out of alphabets to name them, we were in block DB. Most of the houses were overcrowded; a typical family had ten kids sharing one space.

We were a family of eight, my parents and my sisters shared one room. The weather was usually smoldering hot, but sometimes it would rain, and it would give off a fresh earthy smell. We always knew when a storm was on the way, we could smell it.

Running in the rain with laughter. My day consisted of getting water for the family and doing chores. There were no mattresses, we were all in one room, my parents on a brick mud bed, and we slept on the floor with blankets. There was not enough water for showers. We had handmade toilets that were just holes in the ground, but it was dangerous for the kids because they would fall in, especially crawling babies.

People called the refugee camp, *"mahali hagugesa,"* the waiting place, with footprints of generations abandoned from the previous people who lived there before us. Going in, we knew there was a possibility that we could not stay there permanently.

After a long day in the sun, when the sun swallows the horizon is dinner time. We headed home to eat and rest next to my siblings and not feel a thing because my tiny body had passed out in exhaustion, but it was still blissful, *"I was home for the moment,"* even if it was just temporary until we did it all over again the next day, like a temporal loop.

My parents were always the first ones to check our name on the billboard, and I never understood why they came back disappointed. I was terrified of going to an unknown place, I saw change as the enemy.

The day our name finally got posted, my mom asked my sister and I to go check because she couldn't deal with the disappointment of not seeing it up there again, but we were still hopeful enough to want to know. When I saw our name, "MUSA" posted on the board, I panicked and ran home without my sister. When I got back, breathless with fatigue from running in the heat, my mom was sitting in a rocking chair in front of our small brick-brown house. She had a thoughtful expression on her face. The sun was setting on the horizon.

My mom stood up so fast when she saw me that her chair was tipped over. As I got closer to her, her face transformed with so many different emotions: hope, sadness, despair, happiness, and excitement.

"Well?" she asked.

"I saw our name," I mumbled with disappointment.

She was so joyful clapping and in tears, full of happiness and

she said, *"About time we leave this hellhole."*

But I just stood gasping for air, as I started to shake. I was dying inside. I couldn't breathe fast enough to ask my mom,

"What does it mean?"

even though I already knew. I didn't want to leave.

I knew change was coming, the process had already started. My parents had an orientation before leaving the camp, they were instructed, *"You could only take the clothes you are wearing and change of clothes for the next five days, nothing else."* Then, the IOM told them about "San Diego," about toilets inside the house, eww, about inside stoves that lit a fire without smoke so we wouldn't have to worry about teary eyes while cooking. They learned about tall buildings, stairs, and fridges, and my parents talked about how they saw pictures of everything America had to offer.

My parents would come home and tell us everything they learned about our new home since the orientation was only for the parents. Everyone was excited but I was paralyzed with fear, *America? San Diego? I didn't want to leave the only place I called home. Kakuma was my home, my friends, and everything I ever knew. What is waiting for me in this new place?* I wondered.

When my mother talked about San Diego or America in general, she would say, it was "perfect." Life would be so much better, we would never go hungry again, education would be free, houses like a palace, it would be so cold, we would need jackets even while inside. White frozen sand poured from the sky, and even the white walls were freezing. There would be a white rectangle in the kitchen that was full of food, never empty, so we would always have something to eat, and our stomachs would never burn like they were on fire from hunger or wondering what was for dinner.

We wouldn't need gas lamps, lights would be everywhere, and we wouldn't need the moon to see the night either. We would have soft spongy beds for our ribs, we would never sleep on a hard cracked floor again. The outside was full of fresh air, you could feel the breeze, and the air caressed your face like fingers. *"Ya right"* I was skeptical, there was no such thing. It sounded magical.

San Diego, March 2004. We rode in the car for the very first time, racing through the downtown traffic with my whole family into the unknown. It was in the evening, lights everywhere, shining brighter than a lone moon in a desert. Buildings taller than giraffes had me thinking,

"Where was this place, were we going to live up there?" I wondered.

I was numb with fear; height was not my specialty. Lights passed by as bright as stars, the moon was nonexistent, but the night was still as bright as day. I was on my way to my new home with my family, on our way to the uncharted, and the uncertainty of our destination. Thinking about the unknown that lay ahead had me seeing the blur of the glare from all the different lights coming from the giant buildings around me. The cars zooming by.

San Diego was everything my mom said it was, minus the money growing on trees in the backyards of course. Half-naked people everywhere. People that looked like aliens with different skin colors and blue and green catlike eyes. Other than the shock, it seemed my anxiety was unnecessary. It was heaven.

We had spongy beds that we were scared to sleep on for weeks. We had food in our house every day. We went to school a month later. It was torture, being new and not speaking English, but at least girls were allowed to attend school there. We had more clothes to change to every day, we had parks to go to, and toys to play with. We had a box that talked and showed moving images. We lived upstairs and had three rooms with multiple windows as big as our door back at the camp. We had soft mini beds for our butts while watching TV, the weather was very familiar, and it was everything we ever hoped for.

Or so I thought, but America came with rules. We had to assimilate, and blend, which came with identity confusion–being a teenager in America

was a disaster. I was in high school, and I couldn't read or speak English. I had to juggle two different cultural standards, I got in trouble at school for not looking at my teacher and claimed I wasn't listening. At home, my mom yelled at me for making eye contact and said I was defying her.

I had to learn to act a certain way at school to minimize getting bullied for being different and learn to act a certain way at home, so I don't appear too *Americanized* and disrespectful towards my parents. And, to deal with society's expectations. **They didn't teach my parents this part of being in America.**

As my teenage years disappeared, adulthood approached. I learned that not everything is a fairytale with a happily ever after. Our new home came with walls, bans, ICE, and Executive Orders that changed lives; a point of a pen was a weapon here. Our new home came with high rent with no rent control, living paycheck-to-paycheck, feeling unsafe from our authorities, overpriced college education, and fighting for our rights to call America home.

But this is home, for now, we belong here.

-My Puzzle Pieces

From the glaring harsh sun beating down on them

with sweat running down

like a stream in an abandoned forest on their backs

light beams as they plow the acres that

tried to wash the Chizigula out of my ancestors

but they survived in spirit.

While their oppressors succeeded in the introduction of illiteracy.

The erasure of the written Chizigual

is still spoken a hundred years later.

Today I'm relearning the simple art of writing

wee vi hee?[1]

rather than the boring greeting of,

how are you?

that is tattooed on my brain.

I will gladly be amongst the ones with the privilege of relearning.

I don't remember when I started to dream in English.

One minute my dreams are in Chizigula,

dreaming of Dekhaley at the toobu[2] where,

I had to walk five miles to get mazzee[3]

for my family.

I now breathe, talk, believe, and exist in four languages,

but at times they work against me.

They cut me in half and send me to different paths.

At home, I'm my mother's daughter,

I avoid eye contact out of respect,

while at school I am *Society's Famo,*

who knows the rules and the norms of

saying,

"yes" instead of *"yeah."*

I have to pull myself together from the

edge of assimilation and erasure

to remind myself I am two in one.

I'm all.

[4]nemeye Famo and uloyce wango ne wango,

hodahe usola male, hata unatera vihi.

Chizigula na Chigereza chuse.

-My Scent of Home

Kenya:

The smell of nostalgia

with just a whiff of chicken,

and the curry aroma you carry around

that brings back a place and a time long gone,

a previous lifetime.

A place where I smelled the earthy growth of

bananas, corn, mango, and greens.

All too familiar, seven of us filling the house,

following the smell of you,

the delicious smell of bravery

that clung to you like a second skin.

I remember playing all day in the sun, keeping busy,

trying to forget the sounds my stomach would make,

knowing we had one meal a day and it was usually at night,

and coming home to sit next to the crackling fire,

while dinner appears out of thin air,

as if magic.

Even as a child, I knew the reality of our lives,

living in a refugee camp, and yet,

you always managed to feed us.

You would come home from the sun

beating you down all day.

and start mixing love.

I could smell your scent,

a mixture of seasonings.

America:

New beginnings, what we left behind,

an obscure dream,

and yet your scent is the same, the smell of love,

warm like sleep.

The scent of a hundred seasonings

you use it as if you are blending a love potion,

making the best of what little we had,

yet fulfilling.

You brought that scent with you to our new home,

filling my senses.

That smell of corn boiling away,

the scent of fish frying in the evening light,

making my taste buds dance,

the smell so different yet familiar.

I don't have to watch new lines grow on your face each day

knowing you were wondering where dinner was coming from

now I only see the permanent lines around your mouth.

we have a fridge that's never empty.

I'm left anticipating

what scent is going to cling to you each day,

maybe the scent of tomato sauce sizzling,

or the green bananas and beef stew you so favor?

or your golden sambusas frying in a pan,

or the ugali and Sukuma that so remind me of home?

either way,

I know my stomach won't burn with hunger anymore

and there is no place I rather be.

My mother, who smells of home and safety.

My mother who loves with food.

We celebrate food because we know a time when it was absent.

Loving through food was a distant dream, now forever hers.

Now we fight the urge not to waste food,

knowing throwing food is like a knife to the soul,

knowing not everyone is loved that way.

There is an ongoing battle of a hundred mothers,

wondering how they would love their child today

of children wondering what scent will cling to their mother every day.

-My Roots

Gosha / footprints of oppression / roots interconnected from ancestors to mothers to daughters / prevailed / generations of roots watering each other / with knowledge / language / culture / traditions passed down / blossoming into a tree / even though it might die one day/ the roots stay intact / and continue the ancestry of us / old wound unwilling to heal / fragmented puzzles still mending / still here / thriving.

-My Quarantined Soul

My room has always been my safe place

until it became a confinement.

Remembrance of times long gone

stuck in solitude,

in a pattern forced upon me by this illness

the isolation echoes loudly from the walls,

sleep

eat

work

and repeat.

Restricted.

Being home was a privilege

but it consumed me.

In isolation,

as I let the emptiness eat me,

a phantom within my four walls,

with many roles forced upon me.

Lost in work, school, teaching,

parenting, and distancing.

can't tell between dusk and dawn,

it's all so similar.

I missed the warmth of the sun caressing my face

or the cold of winter with its killer frost.

Surrounded by emptiness and silence.

No sight of an embrace,

hugs were dangerous.

We were a house full of people who

didn't see each other except in passing,

we let our rooms hold us, prisoners.

I missed people outside of my family,

but mostly missed connecting with nature,

the isolation echoed loudly,

My nocturnal nature made the loneliness unending,

insomnia is a thing now.

The nights were longer, the days were longer,

the weeks even longer.

What are weekends anymore?

everyday blurred together,

but my introverted nature was still celebrating.

Still blessed,

with a big family, and wholesome,

with a bed and food,

many can't say the same.

-My Love of Kitchen

The kitchen,

my stomach's happy place.

As I set foot inside,

my stomach starts communicating,

the aroma coming from there tickles my senses,

my throat lets me know I ended up there for a reason,

I'm thirsty now.

I stand in the middle of the kitchen,

taking everything in.

The first sound reaches my ears,

the fridge hums like a bird

letting me know,

my strawberries and leftover rice

from last night are in good hands,

something I still can't believe.

I turn in circles taking everything in,

at the rare sight of the empty sink,

which never happens until nightfall

the only time the kitchen is deserted,

now ghostly

because is not dinner time yet.

I look to the microwave,

I'm taken back to yesterday,

warming up the Panda Express my sister

ordered me all the way from Las Vegas.

I reminisce in the power of taking

something cold like the chill of winter

and turning it into the warmth

of a lover's touch within minutes.

Like the waffle maker,

who turns instant mix into a meal,

the slippery ivory mix

that turns crispy instantaneously,

melts on your tongue

with the sugary taste of syrup,

heaven.

The toaster who has the power

to swallow my bread and spit it out,

a golden orange crunchy goodness

that transforms my kids' faces like a ray of sunshine.

The coffee maker. *Ahh coffee,*

she knows how to keep me sane,

the sound of coffee brewing rings in my ears

like a song of the year,

anticipating its warm touch

on my lips as it coats my tongue,

down my throat

like warm syrup that travels to my belly,

sultry butterflies.

lastly, I turned to the stove,

who is not used enough to her full potential,

waiting to be turned on,

all the memories of spices used washes over me

in a warm blissful kiss.

The memory of my mom

teaching me how to make ugali for the first time,

the smell of the many times I burned it until I got it right.

I am entranced,

walking through recollections of the last time

my mother cooked at our outdoor kitchen in Kenya,

my mouth salivating through the remembrance.

Until my kids startle me into awareness

and bringing me back to reality

there is only one reason

to be in the kitchen for longer than 5 minutes

and cleaning doesn't count.

-My Footprints

Searching for the essence of you, breathing life in a foreign land with our footprints.

Like a transparent soul, the rain never stops crying, as we use the moon as a nightlight to see our footprints.

Playing in the straw-like lush grass, leaving behind impressions of where we once resided, full of our footprints. Now in a new place, a place without the echoes of bullets, as the downtown traffic lights the path for the next generation to leave their imprints.

3

-Deceit

Betrayal

like a dreadful decomposed banana splattered on a scorching road,

like a dam erupted and flooded the whole world

like the smell of rotten eggs after a month under the couch

like you had my heart between your hands and you kept squeezing

until there was nothing,

vile.

I never want to experience it again.

-Losing A Part of Me

Every day you dim my light just a little

every day the sun loses its shine a little

every day you break me

and I let you.

-Self-Censorship

One day, my soul grew silent,

my mind strays to mufflers,

I threw my subversion upon the floor,

while I pondered mutely,

there stood a gentle seashore,

the tongue-tie totalitarianism taming me.

I crave the coastal coral ocean,

I want to let out the fire of outrage,

with complete devotion and fervor,

through which came ousting, ousting, ousting

instead, I uncovered the screening within,

fading into that deep darkness,

back into my memories subsiding

to warn me about the cutting fire

but the well floods as the words release.

-Dream Walk For Me

I yearn to sit on your lap again Grandma,

to feel your arms around me.

I'm in deep dark waters full of memories of you,

how I was so close to seeing you in person

but you were gone too soon.

Now I only see you after my eyes close,

haunted by your laughter,

your jokes floating around me in bubbles,

you are in my nightly dreams.

I so wish to

make you a reality

but I do not possess that ability.

I envy your power

to travel in sleep.

I wait and I wait for your visits,

bittersweet

but I will leave the path open for you,

waiting and waiting

for my favorite memory of you.

One moment you were there,

then you were gone.

Footprints

I remember the night before you left Dadaab.

I got a stomach bug,

and I was writhing in agony throughout the night,

so you went outside, and

you got some leaves from a medicinal tree

and you smashed them and made me drink it.

I remember the bitter taste clawing my throat,

but I felt my stomach pain ease as the minutes passed.

That was our last interaction in person,

in the morning you went back home to Somalia.

There was earth beneath my feet,

I saw you every day in my memories afterward.

Your stories transported me to the past,

I saw your life through the words that came from your mouth.

I dream of walking through the steps you took,

when I see cracked ground.

I yearn to feel your kisses on my forehead,

when the sun disappears,

Your face comes back to me, and all is well again

but then my eyes peel open at the feel of the morning rays and the moment flees

you are snatched away from me again

I am back to sinking beneath the dark clouds

of a world without your breath.

-Wyd

I came to loathe the simple abbreviation of the word

"wyd,"

can I even call it a word?

more like letters,

they are like opening a can of rotten worms

long buried beneath the earth,

they say, "Just making sure I still have access to you,"

the chances are they didn't care what I was doing

at that particular moment, they are just making sure they still have access,

that says,

"You are not my main dish,

just making sure you are still my piece of pie"

they have the gravity to pull me backward

as if the weeks of ghosting were my imagination

as they make sure I'm still their fascination.

-Heartbreak

I always wondered why they call it a "heartbreak" How does something made of muscles break?

I never thought I would ever experience it myself, until that day I felt my heart shatter,

my chambers in pieces, I thought I would find the pieces at my feet, but you had them in a chokehold

I never want to feel that kind of agony again, my heart is now on lockdown, you were my oxygen, and now I look at you nonchalantly.

-A Captive Silhouette

Cave Captive

longing to escape

all eyes seeking

ready to be rescued

nobody is coming

alone in despair to the bone

the relentless expectation

in the shadows of the mind

like a silhouette waiting

for the light to dissolve it.

-Phantom Body on Me

Chilly night,

dead silence,

yet feeling the vibration

of the night as my body goes

in and out of consciousness

REM sleep.

Behind my mind's eye,

a dark shadow near the window lurks,

creeping close

can't tell if it's standing still but it's getting closer,

one minute my body is being absorbed by the fluffy mattress,

the next terror takes hold.

Breath stuck in my throat gasping for air

No, no, No!, I scream in my mind,

gravity holds me captive,

as I wait for my mind to give the signal,

my mind unable to send

the message to move my limbs

frozen in time.

My hands and legs glued to the bed,

the imprint of a heavy body pins me down,

please no

being weighted down,

with a ton of weight on top of me.

I can feel the demon's body

like a phantom load

I'm trying to sob but

the sounds are stuck in darkness.

My mind screaming inside,

as my voice abandons me.

A ghost body holding me hostage,

waiting to be released

waking in terror

gasping for breath

sweat a motionless ice.

I pray my eyes stay shut

I strain to keep them closed

my imagination captures his face

behind my eyelids

white cloudy skeleton face

looking down with holes for eye sockets,

hollow eyes.

long jagged teeth,

hand with long claws,

pushing down on my chest,

dark purple tongue,

hot breath caressing my face,

immobile

silent horror.

My eyes shut close,

afraid to conjure it into existence

if it is real, I would never want to sleep again,

knowing the creature was in bed with me,

claiming my soul,

crippling me with fear,

It made me wonder if it will ever end,

or if this is the angle of death,

coming to claim me.

At last,

I am released,

I shower the room with light

but there is nothing in sight

maybe I dreamed it

it was probably minutes

but felt like a lifetime.

-Hollow

Inna lillahi wa inna ilayhi rahi'jun,
to Allah we belong, to Him, we shall return.

Heaven gained an angel but the world is dimmer
without your smile to illuminate it.

Some days,
my denial keeps you here
until my mind catches up to reality.

Footprints

Then,
I remember you are truly gone,
there is a hole that your presence used to fill.

My world stopped the day I found out,
we were never going to run into each other at 50 again.

I knew I never got to tell you this but,
your jokes transformed my life
and made my day every time.

The community feels your absence.
My grief is silent,
but you are grieved by one more person regardless.

Jannah[1] might have gained an angel
but I lost my best friend.
I miss you every day.

-Your Essence

It's slowly dying,

you can feel it fading,

a piece of you dying every day

you wonder,

should you let it wither?

would you let it die?

or would you be fighting alone?

it would be like a rope being pulled on one side,

it's fading,

is it worth saving? I wonder

should you save it from slipping through your fingers?

did you even have a grip on it in the first place?

so many questions gone unanswered

it was never yours to destroy,

just lies.

-Her Fading Hurt

The sky hurts

numb with pain

lonely with the absence of clouds

her heart a melting snow

in the process of wishing on a dandelion

for the transformation of new beginnings

as the hurt grows wings and flies away

-Melancholy

The last time I saw you in person I was 5 years old.

I always believed we would reunite again,

it was wishful thinking on my part,

we were on two different continents,

where day and night are opposites,

I would stay up all night anticipating your call,

you called, and we exhausted your voice

I could hear your soft hoary voice.

The day you were gone,

you craved to talk to every member of the family

you were sick, and we wanted you to rest but

you said you needed to hear everyone's voices,

I had no idea that was you saying goodbye

I had so much to say, I assumed we had more tomorrows.

When your number showed on our phone the next day,

I was bursting with happiness,

lucky I get to hear your voice again so soon.

Mom answered the phone, the speaker blasting,

all we heard was roars coming from the other side

my heart stopped. I recognized the roars of grief

I knew bad was coming, Grandpa, you were not here anymore.

Footprints

You were reunited with Grandma once again,

the whole house echoed with howls, I couldn't move

I was wandering around like a ghost in the shadows

my eyes lacked moisture.

You were gone and I couldn't be angry, you were at peace but

all hopes of ever seeing you on this side vanished.

I was furious at myself for not being able to summon any tears

did it mean I wasn't sad?

I stood under the shower

until I started to shake from the cold

when I went to bed, still the shaking wouldn't stop,

then, I heard a sound that kept going

I wanted the noise to stop.

It would not stop

it was coming from my throat,

I wanted to go back to being numb

anything would have been better.

4

Being A Girl

Sincerely,
-Your Mind.

Dear Memories,

I always wondered why you are attracted to the negative while the good ones are hard to access. Why do I remember hiding under our brick house with my family while the sound of an AK47 echoed around us, as if on repeat? Why can't I remember the last time I saw my childhood crush and what I said to him instead? Why do you haunt me, chase me down, pull me back, and capture me while I try to escape? Trying to take me to that dark place I have been running away from. The place is full of aching experiences passed on from woman to woman. Why do these memories send shivers down the marrow of my bones so much? Why do they give me that prickling sensation traveling up my spine, as if trying to tell me something that I have hidden away deep in my subconscious?

Hopefully, deep down enough they won't creep up. I keep telling myself there are just memories, they can't reach me anymore. I can't give you the power to mentally exhaust me, I am finally free. At least that's what I keep telling myself. Give me the good memories and lock down the toxic ones.

-Her Burning Fire

"You are just a girl," they say

there is nothing "just" about her

she is more than "just" a mere girl

her presence is hard to ignore

her fire luminous

untouchable

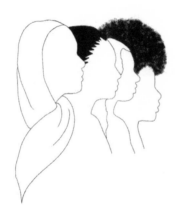

-Bad Thoughts

The mind is a powerful entity seeking to possess

it tries to show me all the bad things that taint my spirit

like a dark angel on my left shoulder telling

me all the bad things I don't want to hear

it belittles me and reduces me into a peanut.

The projections are unstoppable at times

all I dream about is the life outside of me, yet, hey lift sleep from me like I am a victim

like a pellucid soul, floating above me with all the negativity

to weigh me down.

Vomiting insults as tiny as mini glands but deadly.

My mind metastasizes with white-hot fear,

that leaves me disoriented and gloomed,

impulsive and nuisance.

Leaving me seeking relief from my inner torment,

feeling infallible like missiles are being thrown at me.

Vultures invading my brain, coming to devourer me whole,

but it's all in my mind, some might call it being paranoid,

a warning from the mind,

toxic thoughts,

but I fight to stay positive every day.

That's my superpower.

-THAT Uncle

That uncle who is always around

That uncle with no blood relation

That uncle whose DNA is opposite from yours

They wouldn't touch no matter how much he pulled them together

That uncle who is always at your house

That uncle who asks, "Where is my wife?" when you are not in sight

That uncle with a smirk that puts ice water down your spine

That uncle who puts you on his lap like an infant

That uncle who is always too close, his tobacco breath suffocates you

That uncle who demands hugs that last a lifetime

That uncle who makes your blood run away from your body

That uncle who makes your soul flinch

That uncle you are glad you left behind before the hugs multiple

That uncle who taught you the touch of men without your say-so chills your body liquids

Yeah, you know which uncle I'm talking about

-To An Overthinker

Stop overthinking

you spent the night plucking scenarios

that wouldn't see the light of day

stop creating scripts that will never come to pass

you are putting gasoline into your soul

stop hurting your own feelings

-An Illusion

I am lost among the broken bridges

wind through clouds descend from above

frost intentions

freedom without perception, not worth believing

accept me through my darkness

brought forth your tender

-Elegy of Choice

After Sara Borjas

As I walked into the house,

an eerie sensation washed over me.

I observe the house full of familiar faces,

ones I hadn't seen in ages.

Before I even saw my mother,

I knew something was going on

I was not going to like it.

She was facing lines of bags,

caressing a set of deep lustrous

golden-yellow jewelry set,

sparkling in the ambient light.

At 18 years old,

I knew what it all meant,

I have seen it when my sister got married.

I stood frozen and speechless,

stomach rolling with foreboding.

Then, I walked in all the way, knowing

I was next, everyone else was too young

I thought the whispers were just talk, I should have known

now my hands are tied, no escape.

Standing around a pile of my shattered dreams
of thriving, now a fleeting nightmare
my mother's pleading cries ringing in my ears
as begged me to accept the proposal
to become one with a stranger.
Obedience ingrained in my being
it was how it was how it was raised.

My heart cried in agony
dying inside
inch by slow inch
was anyone going to ask if I wanted this? I thought to myself.
I haven't lived yet
I couldn't slow my roaming mind.

There was a quiet curious war brewing
drowning in defeat,
stuck with a promise made
before I could even walk
venom in my mouth
no way around it
it was happening, my heart hardened like a stone
I wondered, *what about love? will I ever experience it?*

A month later,

and was facing the mirror,

glazed lifeless russet brown eyes stared back

eclipsed by nostalgia, I was ready

I guess.

My white dress draped around me like armor

already, I felt the essence of me receding

as they fasten my gold necklace like a choker,

I'm dressed

looking at the mirror one last time

no time for discovery

a day of celebration within a day of sorrow

a little death.

I walked out to face my fate

feeling my roaring fire die out

like an icy winter's night

my future eclipsed by my chosen destiny

ready to playhouse with a stranger

my stranger now,

it seems.

-Red Stain

Finding things out

as they happen to her is a rite of passage

in the art of discovering life for herself

the unspeakable happens

she wished she had known it was coming

duty bound, isolated with him

intertwined

the outcome is in the red stain

for an elder to discover in the morning

to make sure the stain is visible

the absence of it would be

on the 7 o'clock news

her stain was visible

Success!

- The Inner Old Me

Doing chores was the curse of being born a woman, where I come from. I remember as a child cleaning was like a boot camp for creating wives. I would clean every inch of the house, make it shine like pearls, never missing a spot. If I did, I would have to start over. I lived and breathed on getting praised, it meant I did something right but at times. Mom would only notice when things were not done.

Boys never did any cleaning, God forbid you saw a boy washing dishes, even if it was his plate. Mothers were building the next generation of wives and mothers.
My grandmother did the same for her daughters.

Life was lived on expectations, the expectation of learning the wifely duties, to clean, cook, be a virgin, and live under their roof until marriage. Be presentable and acceptable, *A girl will get lost in the duty of marriage,* what else was there? There is no thought of love while being buried in cleaning supplies. And yet it must happen, it's the path many mothers walked, a roadmap to wifehood.
the love I thought I was supposed to get,
when I did what I thought a girl was
supposed to do is not a true formula.

It's a never-ending circle, the love your mom showed you while under her roof is the same love that follows you to your next stage of boot camp, of the dutiful wife. Now you must use the skills collected under your mother's care. *I might as well play dead, in this endless cycle of switching guards.*

-Sleeping Lioness

Inclement fury leaps

the gentle queen sleeps

by the sandcastle

her wrath peaks

as the pokes continue

-People Pleasing

First is,

you are not allowed to notice boys until boys notice you

you now automatically must have a boy in mind, it is time

why are you not getting married? you are too young to get married

you are too old to get married

married, married, married.

Then is,

when are you having a baby? you are getting older,

if you can't have children, are you even a woman?

your baby is too little for a sibling

when are you having another child?

why are you staying in that marriage?

you are getting beat?

After is,

you should leave your husband so he can go have children

you should stay for the kids, the kids need a man in their lives

divorce is haram.

As if that's in the hands of any human being

it is like you are in the business of pleasing the unpleasable

Allah's plan. Live the life you are given

the rest is background noise,

static on a broken radio.

-The Fragments of Me

Somalia,

Kenya,

America,

12 to 34

a mix of confusion, carrying a piece from each,

a journey of isolation among people

who were different from me.

"I don't allow other languages in my class!

Forbidden Kizigua.

Like a broken record in my head,

English

English

English

English.
My mind and soul absorb everything English,

while the other me floats away,

being trained to be voiceless, to silence

Footprints

my mother tongue, linguistic demise

stolen

fifteen years, stealing a hundred years of language preservation.

my ancestors spent a hundred years being oppressed,

but they managed to keep their roots,

and yet, I was losing myself in less than 15 years

why am I erasing their existence?

cutting the umbilical cord that made me possible.

their footprints disappearing in the absence of my language,

being forced to choose between,

Kizigua,

Mai'mai,

Somali,

English,

collecting languages like metals to a magnet and yet being
questioned

every step of the way.

shelving others in exchange for the perfect English,

I learned almost too late to ask, why not keep them all?

who are you?

are you Somalian? Kenyan? American?

My answer having them scratch their head,

my answer having them scratch their head in confusion,

"I am Mzigula."

-Being Born a Girl in Kenya

The minute a girl is born, her life is mapped out every step of the way. Don't play with boys, you will get a bad reputation, and no one will want to marry you when you become a woman. Learn how to cook, so it can be listed as one of your qualities in the long run. Get water from the well. Only girls can do that job and make sure you are the first one there.

Don't be late or the water will shut off and the family will have to beg the neighbors for water and that is unethical. Don't forget to water the garden so it doesn't dry out and harvest any ready food.

Girls can't wear pants or act like a tomboy. Don't dress like a boy, you want people to be able to recognize you and consider you for their son in the future. A lesson I didn't listen to because I was the biggest tomboy, I was allergic to dresses and hair that was done up, until I came to the U.S.

This is how you dress as a woman and still be respectful and modest. Always make sure your hair looks proper, you never want to be associated as the girl with the kinky hair, *but you are the one who does my hair.* I would say this to myself. This is how you don't ask questions about things you haven't experienced yet. You will know the answers to things when they happen to you. It's a rite of passage for a reason.

This is how you prepare to be a wife without knowing any of the details. This is how you cross your legs when sitting down, a lady never opens her legs, don't embarrass me and dishonor the family. You don't want men to notice you, this is how you avoid looking like a victim. Don't give them a reason to notice you.

This is how you learn to wash clothes so you can make sure your husband leaves the house looking fresh and clean. This is how you cook Ugali and fish, so your husband and kids don't go looking for food elsewhere and leave you.

Can't I just learn because it's a basic human need?

This is how to sew anything that gets torn. This is how you eat like a lady. This is how to make sure you look the part, so your husband never leaves you for someone better, *eye-roll*. You can't go to school because you are a girl and everything you need to learn can be taught at home.

A life full of endless lessons, *but what if I want to get an education and become successful in other things?* So, you mean to tell me, you wasted all my time, and you are just going to ignore everything you learned and become a husbandless half of a woman?

Hopefully.

-Still Molding

I know from afar

I might look like I have everything together

but I'm still awaiting completion

5

-The Ocean

I wish I could be like the ocean

alluring and abysmal

calm in her solitude

she knows how to filter toxicity and spit it out.

serene when she wants to be

roars when provoked

while she twinkles and glints

when the stars are sunlit

turbulence

black at night but glimmers blue-green

during the day

celestial

the water intertwines with the sky

as if one

like a Ceylon blue sapphire

how I wish to be her

-The Earth

Vivid

lush, brilliant

a green paradise, giver of life

the mother of us all

vibrant brown, we should take care of her

our collective promise

-The Sky

My sky twinkles at night

the stars wink in unison

illuminating the world

the galaxy's way of saying hello

I mourn the absence of my sky

now hidden in the shadows of tall buildings

I find myself staring

at the absence of her glow

-The Desert

Hot, dry whistling winds

dry baked Earth

like cracked lips

sweating, scorching, glaring

a blazing sea of sand

shimmering in the heat

wind flings sand into their throats and eyes

wildfire

I still miss the sandstorms

it meant I was home

-The Rain

The rain

the last thing my ears hear before

unconsciousness sweeps me away

rain sings me lullabies to sleep

I can smell it miles away as it arrives

rain leaves mud behind that multiplies on my bare feet

rain will never desert me

it followed me from Africa to America

I will always love the rain no matter what sky it's pouring from

rain is my soulmate

even when rain leaves

there is a rainbow left as if to say it will be back

rain may choose to come in anger, but it always washes away my sorrows

to think you used to be my rain

now I only see you through the droplets

-The Night

Peaceful

waiting for dawn

moonlight illuminates the universe

as the moon peeks over the mountains

glistening

nighttime

like a blanket over the world

the time my creativity awakens

-The Sun

The afternoon sun burns the rest of the day away

the warmth of its blaze washing the sins of the day

the day's glaze within the melanin of that one drop of chocolate

as it peeks through clouds smiling upon the people

the burning fire doesn't leave smoke behind

but melts my heart like a candle

glowing within its golden arms winking through my fingers

-The Moon

I remember back home when the moon was full / we would gather around and listen to tales from my mother / but my gaze would stay on the captivating silver light of the moon / as it bathed the world in its gentle embrace / in the velvet night / a radiant sight / it was like a beacon drawing me in / to its soft embrace / brightening the darkness with a tranquil grace / I loved looking at the moon / it was like a silvery orb in the vast starry sea/ guiding the lost / and setting spirits free / a guardian in the peaceful night.

-Mars, Here We Come

She is from the evergreen, where the sun gleams through the emerald forest, everlasting sheen through the acacia trees in midafternoon with pink flaked clouds painted in the background and when it rains, the drops twinkle through the glowing greenish-yellow leaves.

She remembers the air full of life and sweetness as the sun sets with its crimson splashes of dim orange-yellow hues on the horizon, as dusk says goodbye to day, ready to welcome nightfall. At night the moon illuminates the obscurity with the help of stars, and the sky gives an eternal calm with its dusky blanket of warmth.

She went across the universe, existing in the same atmosphere she found the same sky yet different, worlds apart. It wasn't purple or green or red, No! it was the same silvery pale blue of a bright sunny day, or the murky gloomy hue of a shadowy blue sky welcoming her raging storm, opening the heavens with tears ubiquitously.

It wasn't brighter, richer, more vivid, colorful, or moist like the sky she was used to, except for the occasional sunset disappearing into the ocean, a lighter lavender with a creamy orange essence.

In her endless moods. The mornings she is dewy and gold just like back home. Autumn leaves of October are still sublime, timeless, and lustrous. The flowers in celebration of both Summer and Spring share their core with people.

With the sweet aroma of the sea, tickling noses travel down her throat, during high noon. Her royal blue ocean sparkles like a vibrant multicolor lens. Now stuck in a place where nature is disrespected, ire. The silent sea, the carpeted water below with its melancholy swirls is still the same ember in the evening, her welcoming darkness hasn't changed.

And yet it's a different sky because it hurts to breathe, the air is painful. She is suffocating in blackness; the trees are being murdered daily for leisure. Her ocean in agony, going through a soft silent war, weeping tears through weaves.

She sees the attacks coming from every corner, the trees are not defenseless, she can take back her air, the ocean will have enough and finally swallow us whole, and the ground can open and bury us alive. Her sky is the same and yet not, war is brewing, Mother Nature is starting to fight back, stop the attacks.

Enough is Enough! She is not without merit. While furious in rage. She can bring winter fury, her slitting whirlwinds with moaning storms, with shale-gray clouds glomming over the world, with icy breath wheezy its way through her lungs, sucking the air out of existence. Cherish Mother Nature, before she swallows us whole.

6

-To Know You

Knowing you is like dipping my toes

into the ocean

knowing there is a vase space to explore

there is a lot I don't know

but I'm afraid to go deeper

I might drown

-Are you real?

I spent years imagining you into existence

my imagination got the better of me

I made you into perfection

-Yes, You Are

It's okay to say it aloud

say it with me

you are worth it

-Life's Song

The song of life

we write our own chapters and lyrics of the everyday

the puzzles it brings show a bigger picture scattered into pieces

the pieces we are meant to pick up with each year we reach

I'm now picking up the 34 pieces of my journey

life is not made of bright moments

it's made of decisions and paths we choose every day

my night owl fights with the early bird daily

but my journey is a battlefield and I choose to it write every day

-An Empath

This dreadful empathic gift
There are times I wish I could turn it off
it's like swallowing hot coal
feelings too big for my emotional cup.

A connection untapped
a deep thread of undeveloped impressions
just like a hotspot. Senses untamed
absorbing your joy, sorrows, and unpleasantness
as my own, a glimpse beyond the veil
I don't want to feel.

The whispers of every tale
good and bad with each heartbeat
a fragile path I made my own
a symphony of feelings intertwined
in a sea of souls of telepathic currents
that leaves me drained.

That sucks the life out of its surroundings
as it holds the hand of your excitement, fear, and glee
you run away from,
a double-edged sword
no room for my perceptions.
The weight of your pain is sometimes heavy
it seeks strength within the tears you deny
the tears you won't shed
a beacon of compassion misled, a heart like rain

I don't want to siphon off you anymore.
though is if nourishing the land
It is not such a gift since
I don't have room for my own vehemence.

-My Best Friend's Heart

Your mother's infectious laughter and joyful

spirit created an atmosphere

of happiness and mirth.

Her ability to find humor in life's

ups and downs brought ease to all our hearts.

She eased the pain of others

with her captivating spirit.

You always tell me,

Allah loved her more,

and she is finally at peace without pain

Allah gained a wonderful soul.

Your mother lit the world with her glow.

The world is dimmer without her

to chase away the darkness

offering wisdom

with her gentle touch

and soothing presence.

In this time of sorrow, my heart weeps,

I wish I had your resilience.

The absence of your dear mother leaves us hollow,

I can only imagine what it does to you.

She was unwavering in her affection for others.

I remember her on my wedding day,

we laughed until our ribs hurt.

My memory of her was during *the fethese*—gift exchange,

when she attempted to speak English or Italian

or say money in the multiple languages she didn't speak.

The house would erupt in laughter,

my cheeks were on fire from being too stretched with amusement.

I can't fathom the loss of a mother,

or imagine the void you feel in the absence of your other half.

I cannot replace the honey of a mother, but I am here, nevertheless.

I want you to lean on me in your time of sorrow.

Her beautiful memories are forever etched in our minds.

When you start to look around for her, think of all the times she made you laugh.

She was a precious jewel who I miss dearly, and I know you ache for her every day.

She raised an amazing human and I'm thankful to know you.

She's still here in you.

You will see her in your every prayer.

May her memories continue to bring you ease, even in her absence.

-A Declaration

"I love you"

three simple words

a kiss of maple leaf

how I longed to hear them

I received them in writing all the time

as they flash through my screen

I am immune to their effects

the first time I heard them in person

was a whisper in my ear I felt all the way to my toes

"I love you"

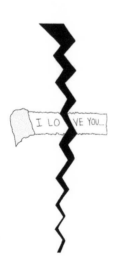

three little words

that revived me and shuttered me at the same time

as they sounded like a goodbye

they weren't mine to keep

-In Your Comfort

I didn't know I was drowning

until you came into my life

saving me while kicking and screaming

trying to hold on

to what? I don't know

maybe just something familiar.

I didn't know I needed saving

until you plucked me out of my comfort zone

change feels like a blanket of the unknown

unprepared.

All that time wasted away in vain

of what could have started earlier

your action of love goes beyond this world

and I didn't know I was seeking

until you found me

in your embrace

I forget my wounds

-Remembrance

I am not a person who lets people in,

it takes me a while to warm up,

like butter left at room temperature,

but I was always all in with you.

Like a film playing behind my closed eyelids

remembering,

the recollections of our time together,

now a distance away,

a smile making my face stretch from cheek to cheek.

You made me feel safe and wanted.

I cannot help but wonder about the times we had together,

what it was like to look into your liquid amber eyes,

the sight of your captivating smile beaming from my phone,

the long talks we had on the phone to nightfall.

Remembrance of your smooth words I believe to be forever,

vibrating from my eardrums to my toes,

but now, just a memory etched in my brain.

How I mourn our time together,

a love once shared,

now separated by oceans in between.

I cannot help but look at the little heaven we were given,

maybe it was just in passing but at least I have the memories to play behind my shut eyes,

do you play them as well? I wonder.

Reminiscence of a world we once shared.

The dictionary says is it the recollection of memories of past events

stem from the Latin word *reminisci,* meaning remembering.

The word gives me the power to tattoo you in my mind,

Where I get to revisit the good times.

The sweet dreams of warm hugs in reminiscing

will you forever be a distant memory?

or is our story still being written?

are you remembering me as I remember you?

or am I living in the shadows of memories long erased?

just a reminiscence of a forgotten nobody.

I don't enjoy going backward so I want you to stay in memories.

-Ode To My Love

My charming love, you inspire me to write

how I love the way you love, kiss, and talk

invading my mind all day and throughout the night

always dreaming about our sunny walk

comparing you to a dreamy remnant

you are most carefree, mystic, and intense

as I plea within this long month of August

in a summertime where the romantics belong

I rejoice in your arms

Cupid's hug.

how I love you, let me count the ways

I love your majestic eyes, smile, and character traits

thinking of your dreamy smile fills my days

my love for you is like welcoming the warmth of heaven's gates

now I must away with my naive heart

and remember my blind words whilst we're apart

-Change

I don't do well with change
I need to get into it gradually
it's like a tidal wave heading to the surface
but this time I sought it out.

Though it might feel like the ocean
welcoming when in it long enough
I still need to dip my toe first.

Change comes with new opportunities
and paths I never see coming
so, I am climbing through the new window
I open for myself.

But still chills my bones and I want to stay bathed in my comfort
then you plucked my soul out of arbitrary
and made me want to face life anew.

My mind had become too independent
and yet I nosedived into you as time stood still
you became my sanctuary
I wanted to bathe in your comfort.
and welcome this new change.

-You Are Here to Stay

Blessed

all her dreams everblooming

coming to life

time goes by, the light from the stars burning on everything she touches,

the moon standing alone in the dim sky with a peaceful reach.

She evolves into a flourishing flower

you are here to stay

from a caterpillar to a yellow-orange butterfly

you are here to stay.

Like one rainy day to the dry dawn that follows

the morning glow comes the warmth touching her skin.

Courage

tomorrow is another day

a new beginning just for her

to feel, embrace, and to outshine.

Like a thirsty earth yarning for a drop of rain

falling into the depths of the beyond

just a figment of her imagination

you are here

to stay.

-Share Your Sorrows

In this dark world, we all bear a weight.

Everyone is going through something,

a burden unseen, a struggle innate, each heart holds a story,

a battle within. Some days you might not want to get out of bed,

but there's hope and strength.

When the world feels heavy, and the skies turn gray,

remember it's okay not to be okay.

We all have a silent conflict we are fighting alone,

for in dimness, we learn to appreciate the light,

and in struggles, we find our internal hue.

Clutch the storms that life may bring,

and water the seeds of resilience to grow,

through tears and trials, we learn to be strong—

and in our darkest moments, we discover where we belong.

We don't have to be strong alone.

Reach out to a friend,

a phone call or text goes a long way.

Share your sorrows, let them see your fears,

even when you want to suffer alone.

Find solace in nature, take a walk outside,

where healing is found

in the rustling leaves and on solid ground.

Let the breeze kiss your cheeks, let the sun touch your skin,

as you breathe in the calm, feel the strength from within.

Look in the mirror, see the warrior under the surface,

the one who's faced battles and found ways to win.

You're not defined by your struggles,

you're defined by the strength that perseveres.

life is a journey, with peaks and falls,

but each valley you conquer, each mountain that calls,

is a testament to your spirit so strong,

a reminder you do truly belong here,

so, when you're feeling low when you're down in the dumps—

know you can rise, like the sun from the slumps,

you're not alone in this unjust world,

with love, hope, and courage, you'll find your way in the end.

Find a friend and unburden your chest.

-Her King

Her innocence in your arms
dark chocolate eyes spiced
with golden flecks stare back at her
veil of attraction
as you promise to adore her.

With Venus' beauty and
Aphrodite's love
flourish, throw back the venom
as you hold her in your arms.

Idyllic flowers of acceptance
deep internal joy
that profound internal energy of
being chosen and loved.

Eclipse with the choice of being the one
Nefertiti's mindset in her spirit
feeling like a queen
red rose opening the sun within
she is yours to keep.

-Love Me for Me

I always wonder if you love me for me

or just the idea of love?

love me for me

not through your image of me.

Love me as a mother loves her child

how the blind would love to see

I am no angel but still want to reside in your heaven.

Love me and never let go

as you tell me

protect me with all your might

as you hold me tight with your warmth.

Love me for who I am, and what makes me, me

like sunshine on a vernal morning through the clouds

as I lay on your warm chest, breathing you in

as the butterflies in my stomach grow wings and make my heart vibrate.

Let me be your other half

as the moon loves to be near the stars

let me rejoice in your kisses as my heart thumps

because you love me for who I am.

-Shrinking

Don't shrink yourself to the size they think you are worth

you deserve the world

stop diminishing to their idea of you

you are a hawk, not a penguin

so, take flight

7

Motherhood

-Growing Life

I didn't find my purpose until I had your tiny soul within me

my body nurturing you into existence

a dance of flavors, like a hormonal show.

My aches and pains, a symphony of discomfort

as my tears flow freely, without reason

as my body builds you.

Growing Life

My joy and excitement intertwined with fear

as belly rounds visible with the sign of you within

my stretch marks, a delicate art to make room for you to bloom

as the days turn to weeks and weeks to months

awaiting your arrival

from your tiny hands stroking my heart within

to having you in my arms.

My symptoms linger with the joy

you will bring as I prepare for you

I bear these signs as we women often do

with the task of creating miracles

a tender glow of growing love from scratch.

-Father of The Heart

My father chose to be my father

he didn't have to

it wasn't because of his DNA

it was from the vines leading to his heart

my father didn't have to be my father,

but he chose me to be his daughter.

He made it,

so I never missed out on the father I never met

he had a spot for me

as an adult, my father still chooses me every day.

I look forward to his "just checking in" calls.

I look forward to his name lighting up my screen.

I don't remember a day without my father being in my life

it would be a dark world without him.

-My Son

My Son, I will move galaxies to stand in the way of foes,

with shimmering eyes,

I reflect on the last thirteen years,

Through trials and triumphs, joy and fears, transcending

I strive to clear the path for you to stand on your own, ascending.

A shield against the world's unjust stare

I am waiting to exhale through whispered lullabies and tender care

in constant fear of keeping you safe in this cruel grayscale.

But I enjoyed the teachings,

to clear a path to navigate life's winding roads

empowering your spirit, nurturing your soul

away to keep secure, a path to decode

a guide to reach your every goal.

Through days of laughter and nights of tears

from your tiny size on my palms

I've witnessed growth throughout the years,

to a young man, I am proud to call my son, my balms.

As a parent, I couldn't be prouder of what I spout,

I want to illuminate a path with sunlight,

to rise above every doubt and navigate a world filled with rage with light.

My Son

Innocence amber eyes full of hope,

raising a black son in this world is crippling,

crushing with fear of dangerous scope,

but the future is rippling,

you are my gold.

-Away From My Heart

Being away from my mother

            is like ripping my heart out

and offering it to the wolves

            while I stand there with a gaping hole

-Borrowing My Mother's Face

the mirror on the wall

reflects my mother's

face as my own

-My Daughters

My daughters, my precious gems.

One, my lucky fortunate, never afraid to voice her opinions

with her big Autumn sunset eyes that see beyond the surface

her name, a successful blessing, destined to be joyful.

The other, my Eve, my emerald jewel

a tree whose leaves a midnight green with russet eyes that sparkle like the stars above

they fill my heart with eternal love. Her laughter, an enchanted melody

smile with that radiant sunlight to illuminate my world, one day at a time.

My daughters, the embodiment of my dreams

with strength flowing like gentle streams

they carry within, a soul so bright

a beacon of hope in my darkest nights.

Their innocence, a touch of the purest bliss

fierce essence, unyielding, never amiss

with hearts so tender, yet unbreakable as steel, the core of my being.

My daughters, the bridge between the old and the new

with every step, you inspire, igniting within me a burning desire

and yet still terrified to raise you wrong.

Bur blessed with the chance to try getting them ready to be their full selves

and make their own footprints.

-Motherhood

I have accomplished many things

but motherhood is my most accomplished task

from the moment of conception,

It is a voyage with threads of purest gold.

As I learned what it means to be a mother

at the age of nineteen,

it taught me what it means to be nurturing,

to form a bond

no words can explain

what it's like to have a mini version of myself.

Motherhood is a gentle touch and a tender kiss

that I will always be thankful for.

In the hush of night, my child's comfort,

in my embrace, listening to soothing lullabies,

through sleepless nights and moments of despair,

yet an unwavering devotion fills my heart.

Motherhood is wiping away every trace of tears,

from the first steps taken, to dreams set free

my guidance, as I teach and shape

a beacon of my strength to see the glint in their eyes.

Motherhood is tending scraped knees and shattered dreams.

Whisper words of wisdom leading through the darkest night,

a big responsibility to uphold,

to solace and grace in this world as I form kind souls.

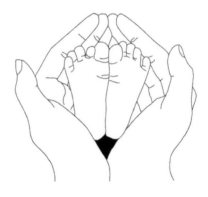

-Dear Mom

Thank you for still holding on to the umbilical cord—

that connected us even when it was severed at my birth.

Mothering me even when I became a mother myself.

My world would be an abyss without you in it.

I got an education as a single mother of two because of you.

You let us explore life while, still in your embrace, in ways, we don't want to let go. You pick me up when I fail just—

like you picked me up as a child when I scraped my knees.

A sunflower is the sun in my palms—radiating your balminess through your children.

We don't say it enough, but you are the best mom anyone could ever ask for. You moved oceans to give us a better life,

your determination is unmatched.

I thank God every day for choosing you to be my mother,

he knew I would need someone like you in my life.

When your call flashes on my screen,

Moyo Wango,[1] my whole body vibrates,

anticipating hearing your honey voice.

You are the only one who ever understood me,

as you are the one who molded me.

My stardust.

-My Miracle Within

It's been nine years since I experienced pregnancy,

I forgot what it felt like to build a small human.

I think God does that on purpose

or the world's population would be lacking

no one would want to experience it again

even now as I write this,

I only remember the good parts

not the nightly tear stains,

or the spinal agony or eight hours of labor.

I remember the creation of love

and music that planted a root

my fatigue informed me

of the life blooming within

expanding my hopes

as months flew by,

the gentle flutter of tiny wings

sang a symphony of life,

as I placed headphones on my belly.

I remember my infinite emotions,

leaving me drained

as anticipation began to creep in

as my body transformed,

it gleamed with the presence of growing life.

I was a sacred vessel that strangers loved to caress

through joy and pain,

the ultimate strife of my body at work.

I remember the bond we created

when you let me know you needed to be fed

my ribs your communication board

in the hushed moments of quiet reflection

I cradled you in my palms soothing,

a melody of grace as you wiggled within my belly.

I remember time lingered with the anticipation of you,

a bittersweet song

as I await your arrival

a precious life,

to become the center of my world

waiting for the day you lay on my chest.

-Stripes

A mark for every day you exist

the room you made your home

vivid purple swirls, the color of bruises

like angry streaks kissing over my skin

you were making a sanctuary for yourself

some might not understand it

and others can't find beauty in it

but it's a reminder of where you once resided

a reminder, I created every cell, every strain,

every fiber, and every bone

they are marks of motherhood, like lightning streaks

a maternal collage, a carriage of your creation

I don't hate them, they gave me you

my ever loving vines, I learned to love

because of you.

-My Mornings Now

The best thing about waking up with the morning rays
is the sounds of giggles and cooing that sounds
like an angel's melody. It's opening my eyes
and seeing that toothless grin shining with happiness
to see my eyes open as if she had been waiting
to see my eyes peel open as if she has been
waiting to find my life force
I am not a morning person but to
hear those musical notes
I will be one for you
my baby girl

-Your Child

When you birth your heart

and they are walking around

oblivious to the dangers of the world

you find yourself getting ready to strike the ground

because your child fell

how dare the Earth move

and gravity didn't reach out

to catch your precious jewel

-Write yourself

I don't see many words written
by someone like me
I want to see myself on pages too
since no one is doing it
I'm going to be the first
I hope you see yourself in my words

Acknowledgments

I am thankful to the editors of the following journals who were among the first to publish some of the prose and poems in their early conception. The People Have Spoken Zine: "Home but Temporary as a "Waiting Room."City Works Literary Journal: "What Makes a Home." and "Own it!" Acorn Review Literary Magazine: "Own it! "City Works Literary Journal: "Mars Here We Come."

This book is for my community, for giving me a place to belong, I wrote this book collection for you, so you can see yourself in my words. A love letter to my people.

To my family: Thank you Mom and Dad for giving me the space to be myself. For helping me raise my kids while I follow my dreams. To my sisters, Binti, Sitey, and Boni thank you for believing in me and for encouraging me to keep going. For helping with bringing this collection to life. To my kids, thank you for keeping me accountable, and asking how the book is going daily. To my nieces, Hajia and Gediya, thank you for your support, your excitement fueled my excitement to get the book ready for you.

To my best friend Amina, thank you for always checking up on me and the progress of the book since you found out about it. Your excitement lit a fire under me and encouraged me to work harder for it to be in your hands. To my best friend Faiza, my sister of the heart. I don't know where to begin. Thank you for all the duas, for the night coffee drinks and car talks. Thank you for the voice messages and the check-ins, and for reassuring me to not give up. To my best friend Isha, my heart. Thank you for being in my life. I admire your resilience and strength. I have always looked up to you. You grab life by the throat, and you never let it bring you down no matter what it throws in your direction, and I love that about you. Thank you for always being there for me. I hope this book helps to take away some of your recent sorrows. I am here for you; you can always lean on me as I lean on you.

To Dan, thank you for helping me keep my dreams alive over the years. For always asking when the book was coming along when I was ready to give up. This book would not exist without you believing in it.

To My creative team: To my editor Kelley, thank you for being on the same wavelength as me and understanding my approach and your power of observation. For making my book come to life. I am excited to work with you on future projects. To my cover designer, thank you for giving my book an identity and making my vision a reality. To my illustrator, thank you for giving my words life and seeing my vision, Masha'Allah, your talent is beyond this world.

To everyone who believed in me along the way. My mentors and friends, Bernadette Johnston, Christina Chomut, Diana Cervera, Cat Coppenrath, Maria Mathioudakis, Bre Neemal, and many more that I didn't name. Thank you for awakening my creativity. For supporting me and believing in me. For being there for me and teaching me along the way. My professors, thank you for always leaving a note on my assignments, telling me "You should write a book," thank you for planting the seed.

To my readers, thank you for picking up my collection and making it your own. I hope it inspires you and helps you navigate this cruel world. To the people who have dreams but are too afraid to follow them, I hope this book inspires you to open your heart to those dreams.

ABOUT THE AUTHOR

Famo Musa is a Bantu poet and artist, born in 1990, she came to the U.S. in 2004. She graduated from the University of California San Diego with a B.A. in literature and Creative writing. Famo has published some of her work in City Works Literary Journal, Grossmont Community Acorn Review, and The People Have Spoken Zine at City College. She also wrote news articles for the Speaks City Heights youth media from 2015 to 2019. She now resides in Houston with her family.

NOTES

Growing Up with Sisters

1. Long cotton east African nightdress

My Puzzle Pieces

1. How are you
2. Well (to get water)
3. Water
4. Is me Famo and my language is mine, you can't take it away from me, no matter what.

Hollow

1. Heaven

Dear Mom

1. My heart

9 798218 376260